True Ghost Stories And Hauntings

Horrifying True Paranormal Hauntings From The Last 300 Years: Creepy True Ghost Stories And Accounts

42/ and

https://www.flickr.com/photos/adforce1/2734097375/

Table of Contents

Like FREE books?

Would you like them delivered to you every week?

Do you like non-fiction books on a huge range of different topics?

We send out FREE e-books every week so we can share our books with the world!

We have FREE books every week on AMAZON that we send to our email list.

So if you want in, then visit the link at the end of this book to sign up and sit back and wait for new books to be sent straight to your inbox!

Introduction

I want to thank you and congratulate you for purchasing the book, *"True Ghost Stories And Hauntings. Horrifying True Paranormal Hauntings From The Last 300 Years: Creepy True Ghost Stories And Accounts"*.

If you are someone who is curious about the afterlife, you will find this book rather intriguing. There are many who will shun these stories about paranormal beings with a lot of cynicism. Then there are others who have lived among them for years on end, in terror.

This book is a collection of real life hauntings that people have witnessed over the last three hundred years. These are recollections of people who have had close encounters with the dead and all of these stories have records to prove their authenticity as well.

If you want to experience real chills down your spine, read on. I certainly had the creeps as I was researching these stories. Some events are so ghastly that they stay with you for several days on end.

No matter how strong or cynical you may be, you should

read this book with an open mind. It is always good to venture into worlds that you know little about, that will make you appreciate the world that you are in at this moment.

I hope this book lets you imagine the journey of all the people whose stories have been mentioned so that you can appreciate your world where these beings simply watch, silently.

That said, you might not want to be alone when you read this book. Needless to say, you might want to keep all the lights on!

Chapter 1:

The Oliver Family Mansion

Who doesn't love a good ghost story? We hear stories about ghastly murders, suicides and several other strange instances when death does not really relieve a person from this world. Instead, these people are trapped in a strange dimension between life and death and are left there to suffer through eternity.

Haunted mansions always have a rather interesting history behind them. The one thing that is common between all these haunted tales is the element of mystery. One such story is that of the Oliver Family Mansion, which is located in a quiet street in Chester, PA.

Home to the Oliver Family, this looked like any regular mansion with large windows, colonial architecture and tall walls. It was quite normal for people to live in huge mansions back in the 1800's especially if they were wealthy. But, in the year 1898, everything changed forever for the Oliver Family.

The whole family went missing overnight. It seemed that they almost disappeared into thin air. Did they pack up and leave the village for financial reasons? Could it be that they tried to escape an old enemy? Did they just move like other regular families? Or, here is a scary thought... did the family leave their beloved mansion at all?

Locals stress the fact that nobody saw the family leave the village. It is a small place where people are quite familiar with one another. Someone must have seen an entire family walking out of the village. People even searched for the members of the family, or perhaps their bodies. But, nothing was to be found.

The family had vanished without a trace, leaving the locals baffled at the thought of what could have possibly happened that night at the mansion. Obviously, everyone has kept away from the mansion ever since. People were convinced that whatever it was, it wasn't of this world.

Like every horror story, this one too had brave investigators who looked for clues and evidence inside the mansion to try and figure out where the family had disappeared to. They were unable to find anything there either. This is one of the strangest disappearances of the 19th century, a mystery that is still unsolved.

And, it seems that we will never understand what happened in that mansion. We have heard of individuals disappearing and never coming back. But, an entire family? All at once? Where did the Oliver Family go after all?

The truth is that they never left the mansion at all. And, they never may. The family may not be physically present in their home but they still hold on to the memories of their beloved home. Locals say that the family is still in the house in spirit, quite literally at that.

Several locals have seen apparitions of family members through the large glass windows of the mansion. They are even to be seen dining together and having a pleasant time with one another as the onlookers watch in complete horror. The family is there and definitely wants to be left alone.

People who have ventured into the mansion swear that they have the creepy sensation of being watched by someone. It almost feels like someone is in there breathing down your neck, according to people who have visited the mansion. Footsteps are often heard and are more intense in certain parts of the house.

Right from the time they entered the gates of this mansion, the locals say that they literally got chills and constantly felt like they were in the presence of something that they could not see but could very evidently feel. And, the members of this family are not pleased when they have intruders in their space.

Phantom activity has been noticed in many areas of this house. The dark walls are full of vibrations as if someone is brushing by them as they walk. Some parts of the house are particularly haunted, especially the upper floors. It is in these windows that people normally see the apparitions of the members of the family.

So, is it possible that something occurred on the upper floors on the fateful night. People can only guess as this is still one of the biggest mysteries in that part of the world. No one has yet found an answer.

Despite the haunting mystery around the Oliver Family Mansion, several brave people have tried to venture into the house and find an answer. In the yesteryear's, when people relied on cameras with films, something strange was found by everyone who photographed images inside this mansion.

When the reel was developed, several ghostly apparitions were noticed in the pictures. The people who clicked these images vowed that they never saw anything while they were still inside the house. But, like everyone else who has been in the Oliver Family Mansion, they also experienced the eerie sensation of being watched all the time.

Like all mansions and castles that were build in those days, the Oliver mansion too has large and heavy doors. These doors would never shut with the breeze or a slight nudge. They needed a good amount of force to close. This is why none of the individuals who went into the house ever ventured in there again.

When they left the house, the door slammed shut right behind them. Locals also say that they have heard doors slam shut now and then; as if someone is telling them all to just stay out and never come back.

When you think about it, this sounds like a tale from any horror story. But what is most baffling is disappearances of multiple people at one time. Our world has witnessed several such strange disappearances over the years. People seem to disappear so easily into thin air. For someone reading these stories, it may seem like yet another urban legend, but for people who have witnessed such disappearances, the memories can haunt them for a lifetime.

For instance, in November 1930, Joe Labelle visited a village by Lake Anjikunji in North Canada. Being a fur trapper, he had made several trips to this village and was quite familiar with the residents. The population of the village was of about 2000 people. He came back one day to see that all the villagers had just disappeared, leaving behind no footprints in the snow or even sled marks.

The grain in the huts of these villagers was untouched. What is eerie is that the sled dogs had been buried in the ice. But, what really made the investigators flee the site was the fact that all the ancestral graves of the villagers had been emptied!

When we witness so many people disappearing with no trace and all in one go, it makes one wonder if we really may be connected to a world beyond our understanding. Can we trust the tales of alien abduction? If not for that, what could these mysterious disappearances really mean?

Did these people that we saw really even exist? How can

we ever tell when our world is shrouded in such mystery. These stories makes one really contemplate every meeting with a stranger. Or worse still, is it possible that we are being watched this very instant by someone from the other world?

The Oliver Family Mansion is definitely one such structure that keeps people on their guard in Chester, PA. The place is so scary that people are afraid to walk passed it even during the day. After years of being abandoned, this Mansion that was once a beautiful family home now stands covered with creepers and weed.

The roof is ready to fall apart and the wood is rotten. Those who watch the house find it tragically gripping. Whether the entire Oliver family met an untimely end or whether they even existed in the first place is something that the locals always talk about with a strange sense of the family still living amongst them.

Chapter 2:

The Story of Bathsheba

Witches have always been that element of evil and fear in all the fairy tales that we have heard about. We imagine witches to be women who fly around on their brooms and make these magical potions. But, when we come out of this imaginary world of witchcraft and enter the real one, it can be extremely frightening, as several people have witnessed in the past.

The Medieval times is known for being an era of notorious witchcraft practices. Some of these witches were burned alive and were put to rest while some lived on, like Bathsheba Sherman.

Devil Worship or Satanism is a concept that we are all familiar with. But, the thought makes many of us shudder, however it is the norm for many. Witches, in particular derive all their strength by worshiping Satan. They go to any extent to please the devil and are part of some of the scariest rituals in the history of mankind.

During the middle ages, witches had gatherings that were known as the Witches Sabbat in order to carry out these rituals and gain more power. A record of these rituals were made by an Italian priest named Francesco Maria Guazzo. These records are based on certain facts that he was aware of and also has some elements of imagination that were added to it.

Some descriptions like going to Sabbat on Flying goats etc. are obviously from his imagination. However, the actual rituals did get quite gory and witnessed human sacrifice as well. The descriptions of the Witches Sabbat state that the most preferred offering was human flesh.

It was eaten by the witches themselves. The bones were made into a special stew that was consumed by these witches to become closer to the devil, and hence more powerful. Most of these human sacrifices consisted of children.

Bread, oil and salt were not allowed during a Witch's Sabbat because the devil despised these things. Human fat consisting of the fat of infants and children who had not been baptized yet gave the witches additional powers like the power of flight. This fat was also used as an ointment.

Using the flesh and fat of children brought these witches closer to the demons and also allowed them to interact and even be carried around by these dark forces. These Sabbats were long and grueling rituals that usually commenced at midnight and ended by dawn.

Many tales suggest that the devil himself was present at all these Sabbats in the form of a goat. People were possessed by demons and sacrificed themselves to Satan. And, all the Sabbats were held in areas that were quiet and isolated. They were located around mountains and forests where people could not witness them too easily.

The area was pretty much like the Arnold Ranch where Bathsheba Sherman worked and silently served the devil. Bathsheba Thayer, later known as Bathsheba Sherman was a very beautiful young woman. Men fell in love with her and women envied her beauty.

Born in 1812, this young lady often claimed that she was related to one of the witches who was executed in the Salem Witch Trials, known as Mary Towne Eastey. This is one of the many reasons why the locals believed that she, too, was a witch who practiced several Satanic rituals. Unlike several medieval witches who were falsely accused, Bathsheba Sherman was not.

She married a rich farmer in the year 1863 and moved to the Arnold estate. Now, it is uncertain if she lived here all her life or moved to the Sherman farm, close to this vast estate, a few years after.

But what everybody knew for certain is that she lived a very tragic life with all her children dying before they were 4 years old. Some records state that she may have had a son who lived on for quite a few years and worked as a farmer.

These records also state that she had three more children, one girl and two boys who had died under mysterious circumstances. Now, whether these records are true or not, is still a topic of debate.

The accusations about her being a witch grew when people discovered that a child in her care (records do not indicate if it was her own child or the child of her friend) died very mysteriously. When the body of the child was examined, it was seen that a sewing needle had been driven through the skull of the child.

There was no evidence to suggest that the crime was committed by her. However, the court of public opinion found her guilty. What is most baffling is how Bathsheba died. Some believe that she hanged herself after she was accused of murder. However, several articles suggest that in the year 1885 (the year she died), Bathsheba simply turned to stone.

A note was made by the coroner after burying her. This note stated that he had never witnessed something like that. It seemed like her body was completely turned into stone. Some also think that this was a very strange kind of paralysis that even gave the doctors who examined the body a terrible fright.

The body of Bathsheba may have perished in any way that the people describe but what is true is that her spirit assumed the form of an evil poltergeist that would soon become a nightmare for the families that lived in the Harrisville Mansion on Arnold farm. Bathsheba never forgot who her true master was and neither would anyone who came into that house after the ill fated death of Bathsheba Sherman.

Bathsheba lived on as a vengeful demonic spirit on the Arnold Ranch. She followed one pattern of possession. She usually possessed mothers to make them sacrifice their own children to please Satan. She chose her victims quite carefully and it was usually just one person whom she chose in a family to torment.

Those who have seen the spirit of Bathsheba recollect it with horror. One person who lived on to tell of her encounter with Bathsheba was Carolyn Perron who we will talk about in the next story. Her face is one feature that all her victims remember very clearly.

It resembles a beehive that had shriveled up. This ghastly face was covered in cobwebs and did not have any human features. The eye sockets and the crevices in the skull had vermin crawling out of it. The skin seemed to be etched with marks and creases.

Now, if one were to believe in the story that Bathsheba had, in fact, hanged herself, the next bit of description offered by some of her victims would make a lot of sense. Her head seemed to almost lean on the torso over a broken neck. Her head had turned gray and had a peculiar rounded shape.

However, there are other tales of a freakish paralysis that many believe. The vision that most people presented of Bathsheba can seem quite unrealistic and unnatural. However, the fact that they all said pretty much the same thing makes you wonder if what they all said was, in fact, true. And, if it was, the Bathsheba demon was definitely no ordinary one.

Bathsheba was not a regular poltergeist who only scared the inmates of the house that she haunted. The recollections of the residents of Harrisville show us that she was, in fact, the culmination of several evil forces. She was cruel to most of her victims.

This is one trait that she carried back from her living world. Even when she was alive, Bathsheba was known to torment the staff of the ranch for the smallest errors and mistakes that they made.

Bathsheba always kept an eye on her victims and knew what their greatest fears were. Carolyn Perron recollects how Bathsheba used her fear of fire against her. In order to drive her out of the Harrisville Mansion, Bathsheba threw lit torches against her bed.

During these episodes, Carolyn remembers a rather reverberating voice that said, "Get Out or I will drive you out with death." Many people who tried to live in the Harrisville Mansion had to flee! They were actually scared to death by this demonic entity who was clearly upset that they had invaded her space, her sanctum where she had worshiped Satan himself.

14

The attacks on all the victims in the Harrisville Mansion grew more aggressive with each passing day. Those whom Bathsheba had haunted were slapped, scratched and pinched. Objects would come flying at them at great speed. All Bathsheba was interested in was to induce pain to her victims.

All the women who lived in that house recollect the atrocities with great horror. Carolyn Perron suffered the most and suffered the longest. She is believed to have bruises and wounds all over her body. Some of them, she did not even remember how she got in the first place.

Most women who lived on the estate were unable to endure the pain for too long and ended up killing themselves. Carolyn Perron who was one of the most well known victims of the Bathsheba demon endured unexplained atrocities. On one occasion, she found that a needle had been driven into her leg.

Quite like the needle that she had driven into the skull of the child she had sacrificed. This was one instance which confirmed that Carolyn had indeed been, possessed by Bathsheba. After this the family sought the assistance of paranormal experts and were able to exorcise the spirit

Max Mason Hunter

from the body of Carolyn.

The Arnold Ranch, however, is still considered to be one of the most haunted places in the world. It is considered to be home to several paranormal activities. This mansion on Rhode Island has been abandoned for several years now.

There were a few families who did try to live in the house but were forced out by Bathsheba. Whether she was really a witch or just a very tormented soul, we will never know. But, what the stories tell us for sure is that Bathsheba is not exactly a welcoming host.

Chapter 3:

Manila Film Center

In the south western region of the Philippines Cultural Center, the Manila Film center stands tall with its trademark edifice which reaches down to 120 feet below the ground. This magnificent structure is culturally very significant in Manila as it is where the First Manila International Film Festival was held in the year 1982.

This building was an effort to improve the appreciation of films and world culture in the Philippines. Besides being the official national film archive, there is an interesting urban legend that has made this film center quite popular across the globe.

The Manila Film Center was a grand project that was led by the first lady, Imelda Marcos in the year 1981. A group was formed to conceptualize this building and add various components to the structure.

Some of the most interesting elements of this structure included a 360 degree theater that takes the audience through the history of Manila, a Film Archiving Center that specialized in Digital Storage and an Information system for films, a Laboratory for Film making and blow ups and several other minor components.

The concept was extremely futuristic and creative but was not exactly easy to accomplish. It required several thousand workers to put in their efforts non stop - 4000 workers worked 3 shifts. Jobs that normally took six weeks were completed in just 72 hours. So the fatigue and the stress began to take its toll on the staff and the individuals who were involved in the project.

They were in a rush to finish the project in time to host the Film Festival. This rush would end up doing the Film Center more harm than good. When the workers were pushing through the project at 3 am on 17th November the scaffolding collapsed and several workers were buried under the cement that was drying quickly.

They waited for official statements to be made before any rescue or search operation was permitted. Eventually, help came to the ill fated workers after 9 hours. These were 9 hours of suffocation, pain, anxiety and perhaps anger.

The project was very ambitious; so ambitious that the

creators did not really care about the plight of the workers. When the scaffolding fell, first lady Imelda Marcos ordered that more cement be poured on the accident site instead of stopping the work. Close to 160 workers were entombed while they were still breathing!

These souls were trapped in a world they did not belong to. Several individuals have reported paranormal activities in the Manila center. Voices and sounds have been heard on multiple occasions. Some of the angry workers who waited hopelessly for rescue have assumed the form of poltergeists who drove the tourists and staff away.

The situation was so terrible that in the late 90's the authorities had to seek some assistance from a group of ghost busters known as the Spirit Questors. This group visited the Manila Film Center often and tried to contact the souls of these workmen and appease them. While several spirits have left the space and moved on some of them still hold on to that fateful night when they were buried alive beneath the cement.

The building was abandoned for a long time due to the activities of these spirits. However, it is currently again in use. Some say that the building was abandoned after the earthquake of 1990 made the building unstable.

Urban Legend or not, the activities within the Manila Film Center had got the better of all the locals who simply refused to enter the building. No work could be resumed because people were too afraid to go into a building where the bodies of many workers remain buried even today.

One incident that sent alarms of panic around Manila was the death of Betty Benitez . She was in charge of the whole project. Her bizarre and untimely death was soon linked to the incident that took place at the Film Center. She was driving to Tagaytay with a former President of the Philippines, O.D. Corpus.

Now, what is not clear is why these two people were driving together so late at night. On their way, the car went off the road and crashed into a large tree. While Corpus survived almost untouched, Betty died instantly.

People were convinced that his had something to do with the angry spirits of the Manila Center and, therefore, the popularity of the space was affected. People did not want to go in even to see films. This, obviously, put the ambitious Imelda Marcos into a quandary.

She even called in a medium to see if they could

communicate with the spirits of the workers. Something strange happened to him. He went into a trance just a few minutes after he entered the building. The medium who was only able to speak in a local dialect until then, spoke in good English.

He said, according to the records, "Betty is with us. There are 169 now." And, 168 workers were killed in this tragic accident. The activities of these souls do not end at the Manila Film Center alone. They are also known to lurk around the space.

One story narrated by the locals confirms this. A passer by was once approached by a stranger who gave him a calling card. He requested the passer by to call his family and inform them that he was alright. The passer by did call the man's family only to hear the startled voice of a woman who told him that her husband was one of the workers who had been killed in the accident.

In the year 2001, restoration work began in the Manila Center. Several theater shows were also staged there. The urban legends were slowly erased from the minds of the people. But, success did not last long at this center with people choosing other spaces for shows and even to watch films. It is believed that the lack of success of this ambitious project can be attributed to the curse of those who had died a very tragic death.

A documentary was shot in the year 2005 and attempts were made to retrieve the bodies of the buried workers. All 168 bodies were found and given decent burials. Out of 168, not more than 15 had died on the spot. The rest, suffocated and awaited death slowly.

Whether it is possible to appease the souls of innocent people who suffered to fulfill greed and ambition, we cannot tell. Were good burials enough for these souls? Are they still out there looking for peace? Or, could they be out there seeking revenge?

Chapter 4:

The Perron Family

Harrisville on Arnold Farm is one of the most sensational horror stories of our times. The film "The Conjuring" is based on the haunting of the Perron family who have witnessed the most ghastly incidents during their 10 year long stay in the mansion with the entire family.

The exorcism of the Bathsheba demon is considered to be one of the most horrific ever witnessed by paranormal experts Ed and Lorraine Warren. Roger and Carolyn Perron wanted to move to a quieter location where their children could enjoy the peaceful country life.

This is when they were able to get a great deal on the Harrisville Mansion on Rhode Island. Considering their financial condition, this was one of the best things that could have happened to the family, or so they believed.

In 1970, the family purchased this old house on an estate that spread across two hundred acres. It had a large barn and even a farmhouse. It seemed to be the perfect place that the children could explore and grow up on. But, on the day the family moved in, they were given a very cryptic message by the owner. "Leave the lights on at night", he said.

This was the beginning of a journey that actually took the family through various dimensions of space and time; many that they were never able to get a grip of. And some that the family refuses to talk about even to this day.

The estate was old and had been home to several generations. People had lived and died on this estate over its time. Some of these deaths were unfortunate. For instance, 93 year old Mr. John Arnold had hanged himself in the barn. Some people died of poisoning.

There was also the tragic murder and rape of an 11 year old child that has not been solved to date. Two people had drowned in the creek nearby and four of them had frozen to death. These spirits had not been completely put to rest and still claimed ownership over the land and the house.

The Perron Family was now aware of why they had been told to keep the lights on at night. This family with five little girls, literally lived among the dead for a long, long time.

The Perron family learned to live with these spirits as they seemed to be quite friendly in the beginning. For example, some spirits were just around the homestead as opaque apparitions. Others interacted with the family and loved them. One of these spirits smelled like fresh flowers and the other one loved the children and actually kissed them good night, according to the records.

A spirit of a young boy often joined the girls at play time and amused them by propelling their toys and pushing them around. Some of these spirits were also welcome in the house. For example, a female ghost took care of the chores for the Perrons every once in a while.

She would sweep the kitchen clean and leave a pile of dust on the floor for the family to sweep up. She would make sweeping noises in the kitchen but the Perrons did not mind one bit as she did not harm the family. The only thing that the family talks about is that the broom would never remain in one place. It would always be placed in a different spot in the morning.

The spirit of Mr. John Arnold also lived among the other ghosts and the family. He was called "Manny" by the family and was just as harmless as the other apparitions in the house. He would just appear out of the blue and watch the children play.

The children recall his crooked smile and how he would just disappear if any of them made any eye contact. He just seemed to come by each day and amuse himself watching the children playing and exploring the farm. Only the children were able to see Manny but they never had a single interaction with him.

Along with meeting these rather cheerful spirits, the Perron family also had their share of scary paranormal experiences. Objects levitated right before their eyes on some occasions. Beds would float and telephone receivers would just slam on to the bases sometimes.

The guests of the Perron family witnessed poltergeist activities like doors slamming, chairs sliding out from under an unsuspecting person. Objects would glide across the floor as they watched in horror. Some guests also mention how pictures would crash down onto the floor from the walls.

Some of them even saw blood oozing out of images and even from the walls. A perpetual bad stench spread all over the house and would become more exaggerated at times.

People also vouched that they always felt like they were being watched.

But not all the spirits were as welcoming of the Perron Family as the other ghosts. There were a few demons or evil spirits that tormented the children and their parents to great extents. Some of these experiences were so horrifying that the Perrons who live on just won't talk about them. Questions about these incidents are either left unanswered or are just answered in a puzzle.

These spirits would target the little girls often. They would be shaken out of sleep in the middle of the night. Their hair and legs would be pulled roughly while they were asleep. The front door of the house would often slam shut with great force. It was so strong that the house would shake.

They also witnessed doors that would freeze and not move. It seemed like someone stood there and held on to the doors tightly. No matter how much force Mr. Perron applied, it seemed they could not get the doors to budge an inch.

There was one entity that screamed and ran around the house. It kept the family awake for nights on end screaming in an eerie voice, " Mamma!". When Cindy

Perron was 8 years old, she was too scared to sleep alone.

She always crept in with her sister saying that she heard scary voices and when her sister asked her what the voices said she replied, "There are seven dead soldiers in the walls". The house had witnessed seven generations often filled with some very painful deaths. The spirits were possibly warning the children about the times to come.

The family also saw the spirit of a 4 year old child who was often spotted in the hallways, crying and looking for her mother. This spirit visited Cindy often and she even recollects sharing her toys with the spirit of this little girl.

There was one spirit that was exceptionally evil. It was the spirit of a former male resident on the estate. In the accounts of the hauntings at Harrisville Mansion, the family hints that the spirit may have sexually abused the girls.

This is one incident that none of the girls ever talk about. In one interview Andrea Perron dodged this question and replied, " Let's just say that there was a very bad male spirit in the house - with five little girls."

The worst of the them all was the spirit of Bathsheba

Sherman. She was known to be a bitter woman who had murdered an infant by driving a nail into his skull. She was believed to be a witch who had died a very unnatural death.

It seemed like her body simply froze and turned to stone. Now, Bathsheba was after the children. She usually possessed the mothers in the families, forced them to kill their own children and eventually kill themselves.

Bathsheba always had one victim and in the case of the Perron family, her victim was the mother, Carolyn Perron. The family recollects that whenever Bathsheba was present in the room, a strong stench permeated the space and it seemed to seep into the walls and make it impossible for them to stay there. Bathsheba wanted Carolyn Perron out of the house but she desired Roger Perron.

There were several instances when things fell down to the ground and broke. Roger Perron would take them out to the garage and try to fix them. That is when he would feel Bathsheba touching his neck gently, breathing on his neck and caressing him. This was one of the many reasons why this spirit loathed Carolyn Perron and tortured her endlessly.

The first encounter of Bathsheba and Carolyn Perron seems to be straight out of a horror flick. Carolyn Perron woke up suddenly one night, just before it was dawn to find an apparition at the foot of her bed. She describes the apparition as a woman with a shriveled up face and a broken neck that hung to one side.

She wore a gray dress and was quite ominous in her first message to Carolyn Peron. She said, " Get out or I will drive you out with death and gloom." And, until Ed and Lorraine Warren came to their rescue, Bathsheba kept to her word.

Carolyn Perron was tortured at the hands of Bathsheba who literally pinned her down to the bed and banged her head against the post, demanding that she leave the house immediately. While she would be busy with her chores in the kitchen, Carolyn would feel a sharp slap across her face. She was pinched and beaten until her body was covered in bruises.

The attacks only became more aggressive with time. Carolyn's leg was pierced with a large needle when she was lying down on the sofa on one occasion. Her body grew weaker and the fear of being attacked with no warning kept Carolyn on her guard all the time. When her attempts at scaring Carolyn out of the house failed, Bathsheba tried something more horrific.

She possessed her body and invaded Carolyn from inside; something that she just could not escape from. She never discussed the things that happened to her, Andrea and Carolyn Perron recall. But everyone in the family knew that Carolyn was suffering outrageous things in silence.

The Warrens

One of the friends of the girls recommended that they consult experts about the experiences that they were having on the estate. She spoke to them about Ed and Warren Lorraine who had been involved in some extremely important exorcisms and hauntings.

The couple had traveled the length of the country to help people cope with the paranormal activities that they had been witnessing and experiencing in their homes. They were experienced paranormal investigators who would be able to put the family's suffering to an end.

The Warrens often spoke about their experiences and shared them with the public. In one such public speaking workshop, the girls met the Warrens. Seeing the desperate situation of the girls, the Warrens decided to help them.

31

When they visited the Warren's house, Carolyn Perron had been completely possessed by Bathsheba.

They were asked to investigate several areas of the house where the paranormal activities were at their peak. Ed and Lorraine did notice several spirits in the house and were baffled at the power of some of the evil spirits on the estate.

The film, "The Conjuring" shows that the spirit of Bathsheba was successfully exorcised from the body of Carolyn Perron. However, in reality, the night of the exorcism took a rather unexpected turn and got completely out of control. The Warrens were unable to control the spirit of Bathsheba.

Roger Perron who was already aseptically of all the incidents in the house asked the Warrens to leave the estate immediately. The relationship between the Perrons and the Warrens did not end well. But, according to the statements of Ed and Warren Lorraine, they had never witnessed anything as ghastly and evil as the haunting of Harrisville in their 50 year career.

While Ed Warren has passed away, Lorraine Warren still maintains records of the investigations that they carried out at the Perron family home.

The Perron Family lived in the house for 10 years after the night of the exorcism. They were severely hit by the recession and were financially unable to move out of the house. When they finally moved out to Georgia, they learned that several people had tried to purchase the Harrisville mansion.

One family even hired a contractor to renovate the house. But the contractor fled the area, screaming and shivering. He even left his car behind. Currently, the house is owned by Norma Sutcliffe. She and her family have also witnessed instances when furniture would vibrate, sounds emanate from the walls and the doors would slam shut. They have also seen an elderly woman walking around the house, silently. However, nobody witnessed anything as horrible as the Perrons did.

Andrea and Cynthia Perron

Andrea and Cynthia Perron, the daughters of Roger and Carolyn Warren shot to fame when the film," The Conjuring" was released. They were interviewed by several people who were curious to know what actually happened in that house for the ten years they lived there.

Cynthia Perron recollects how their toys were often targeted by poltergeists. The girls would arrange all their toys to play and if they went away even for a few minutes, they would come back to find these toys broken or completely messed up.

Sometimes, the girls would just think that it is one of the sisters playing a prank on them. However, what they never understood was the same incidents when they were all alone in the house. How could that be a prank?

Hide and seek was one of the girls favorite games. Andrea remembers one instance when Cynthia went into the barn and hid in a wood box that just had a lid over it with no latch. After 20 minutes, she figured that no one could find her and that she should just get out.

But, the door just would not move. She was stuck in the wood box which was made of oak, suffocating, kicking and screaming. When she was about to give up, her sister Nancy came in and helped her out of the box.

Cynthia clearly remembers the first time she saw Bathsheba. A lady in a gray dress, with her head hanging to one side of her neck walking towards her with her arms open. A very frightened Cynthia ran out, screaming and fell off the stairs in her frenzy.

She remembers that her mother came just in time to break her fall. Since that time, Cynthia heard Bathsheba all the time. And these voices were not just in her ears, they played in her head constantly.

Andrea, on the other hand, speaks very less about the instances. She said that they always lived in terror. The mansion was huge and had about 24 doors. Every time the door creaked or the latch moved, they could never be sure if it was one of the family members or something that they hoped it wasn't.

To escape this terror, Andrea always stayed at school, with her friends. Only after 30 years, after moving out to Georgia, she mustered the courage to write a book about the haunting experiences in the house. Three volumes of the book titled, "The house of Darkness" explain the horrifying struggle of the family while they were the only living among the dead.

Making of the Film

"The Conjuring" which is based on this story was filmed on a set that resembled the haunted mansion. However, this set too had its share of eerie experiences. Once the family decided to visit the set. Only Carolyn Perron stayed at home because she just thought that it was too much to handle.

The family was asked for a joint interview when they visited the set. They agreed gladly and just as they were setting up, a strong wind came right at them. Everything on the set went flying around. The wind was at a speed of at least 70 miles per hour. But what baffled everyone on the set was that nothing around them moved an inch. The girls recalled Bathsheba's curse. At the same time, Carolyn Perron had a fall and broke her hip.

She was taken in for surgery the next day and the family was waiting for her to come out of the sedation. Andrea recalls that just for a second, Carolyn sat up bolt straight, looked at her, whispered " Bathsheba's Curse" and went back to sleep. She slept through the entire day and was unable to speak to the family members for several hours after that.

Andrea and Cynthia Perron say that the memories of the house will never leave them. Even while writing her book, Andrea had to cope with nightmarish memories. It was not an easy book to write, she recalls. However, it was also very liberating. She shared some of her worst memories about the house.

There are several sights, sounds and smells that bring the memories gushing back. The family has moved on and grown but this haunting is one thing that they cannot forget. It has made them who they are. Would you be able to forget ten years living in place where you did not know what was on the other side of the door?

Chapter 5:

The Iulia Hasdeu Castle in Romania

Sometimes, we're are unable to separate ourselves from the memories of our loved ones. We frame pictures, write songs or just keep them in our thoughts to make sure that they are with us even when they have crossed the realms of the living world. It is said that parental love transcends everything mortal.

This monument is an example of the love that a father had for his daughter. He kept her with him even after she was gone and made sure that her memory lived on for the world to see.

The Iulia Hasdeu Castle is a fascinating monument that stands in Campina, Romania. Many travelers have been intrigued by the legends that surround this building and the sheer grandeur of the castle. They have researched in great depth about the history of the Iulia Hasdeu Castle to discover the connections of this space with paranormal beings.

This is a space of great spiritual and paranormal significance. People who have visited it cannot overcome the haunting beauty of the structure and the tragic history that it is surrounded by.

Originally built as a folly house, this Castle became a landmark in Romania. Bodgan Petriceicy Hasdey built this castle to the memory of his daughter who had met an untimely death. It took three long years to complete the project and it was then blessed by Bishop Ghenadie Petrescu Arges.

Iulia Hasdeu was Professor Hasdeu's only daughter. She had a bout of tuberculosis that claimed her life at the tender age of 18. This incident shook her father and broke him completely. He had lost his beautiful daughter who was loved by everyone, including her teachers and friends.

Iulia was a smart girl who was considered a child prodigy that everyone mourned when she died. She was extremely interested in music and did rather well in the field. She was a student of the Sf. Sava and Music Academy, where she mastered the piano and vocal skills.

She then continued her secondary education in the Sevigne

College of Paris, where everyone was in awe of the young girl. She was exceptionally talented and highly intelligent. She mastered seven different languages by the time she was 16 years old. She was not just another girl with a great aptitude for languages.

She pursued fine arts, learned to play the piano, sang and even performed in the theater. She has several poems and plays to her credit. When she was just 16 years old, she pursued various courses at the School of Higher Studies. During that time, she also attended the Faculty of Letters and Philosophy at the La Sorbonne in Paris.

Three volumes of these priceless creations of his daughter were published by Professor Hasdeu under the title of Hachette. It was no wonder that her death brought a lot of grief to anyone who was associated with her for even a brief period of time.

Professor Hasdeu constructed a temple to honor the memory of his daughter. However, this structure was vandalized by people who believed that Professor Hasdeu was a Satanist. He was a bereaved father who wanted to communicate with his daughter.

He made several attempts to do so as a result of which he

was labeled Satanic. Several years later, the structure was restored and converted into a place of tourist interest. It is also the most visited place in this part of the world.

Now, Professor Hasdeu has one single objective in his mind. He wanted to be able to communicate with his daughter. For this, he constructed the Iulia Hasdeu castle with so many details and symbols that you can feel the vibrations from the time you enter the space. In the year 1983, the professor and his wife spent the summer in Campina where he became interested in a piece of land that was around a property owned by his friend.

He decided to buy this place and create a castle that was only meant to for conversations with his daughter. Professor Hasdeu practiced spiritualism that helped him actually talk to his daughter's spirit. Spiritualism is a concept that explores the relationship of spirits with the world that we live in.

This is a concept that has reached several countries today. The idea is quite simple, we are all essentially spirits that are immortal. Our bodies are only simple mediums that allow us to exist in the world. This medium allows us to learn and grow intellectually.

This concept also states that spirits can influence our physical world in a direct or indirect way. They can be active or passive, but what matters is that they can be a part of our world and we are a part of theirs.

Professor Hasdeu embraced spiritualism as the only way he could stay in touch with his daughter. He claims that during these sessions, Iulia was actually able to provide plans for the construction of the building. These plans were very strongly influenced by numerology and included the magic numbers 7 and 3 in several ways.

For instance, the building consists of 3 underground rooms and 3 towers. The stairs consist of 7 steps each. This is something that Iulia had mastered and delivered to her father during the sessions of spiritualism. These messages were transmitted all day and night. They were mostly in French.

Professor Hasdeu dedicated his life to the practice of spiritualism. He recollects the first time that he ever had an experience with the spirit of his daughter. He was just sitting at his writing desk all alone when he felt s number of short, sharp raps at his temples. It almost seemed like a telegraphic code.

Then, with no voluntary effort, his hands moved, picked up a pencil and began to write on a piece of paper. This happened for a few seconds and when his hand stopped writing, the professor felt like he had come out of a deep slumber. The message on the paper said, " I am happy, I love you and we shall see each other again. This should be enough for you, Iulia".

It seems like even death could not separate the girl from her father and she had to come back to talk with him. There may be someone that we have loved and lost. Someone whose final message we all yearn for. But, will we ever be able to get over the fact that they are communicating with us from the world of the dead? You will never know till you experience it perhaps.

For the next three years, Professor Hasdeu took instructions from his daughter to continue the construction of the building. One can attribute the details of this castle to the genius that Iulia was. The main door which is made of stone stands on a delicate diamond bearing.

This makes the door very easy to open despite being so heavy. There are grids painted on the doors in the castle to symbolize the sun. The windows have several symbols of spiritual significance painted on them.

The inside of the castle consists of grand colors and frescoes. There are several rooms within the walls of this castle. One is the living room that consists of several family portraits and has beautiful carvings on the wall.

A tower on the right consists of a scholar's room. But, the most significant room in this building is the room dedicated to the spiritualist sessions that professor Hasdeu had with his daughter. This room is exceptionally quiet and has blackened walls to enable the spirits to communicate effectively.

In this room there were several symbols like the angel's head, triangles and even butterflies. Professor Hasdeu used written communication as the first medium. Direct automatic writing like the one in his first encounter with his daughter formed a major part of the communication.

In addition to that, several ectoplasmic images were taken during these sessions. These images and writings are put up for display at the castle even today. You will see that the questions are related to Iulia as well as the Professor's father and grandfather.

Sometimes, a cultured medium was used to receive clear signals from the spirits of the departed. The symbols, the writings and the images are proof that this place was a center of great paranormal activity. The story of the communication between a bereaved father and her daughter is definitely heart wrenching.

This house was made with such love for Iulia that she still walks around the castle. People have seen the apparition of a young girl holding daisies, walking in the garden. Several visitors have heard the piano playing beautifully, accompanied by a haunting voice. Perhaps, Iulia still longs to talk with her beloved father.

Did they meet in the afterlife as Iulia promised in the first writing? If they did, is this castle the place that the family still calls their home?

Chapter 6:

The Spaghetti Warehouse

This Italian joint has been proclaimed the most haunted building in America. Houston is home to many haunted places, but the Spaghetti Warehouse, which is functioning even today has a lot to offer to the people who make their way there for a fine dining experience.

Most of the haunted stories in Texas will tell us about family vaults that are home to bodies of people who met mysterious ends in their own homes. But, the Spaghetti Warehouse is an entirely different kind of story that is sure to send chills down your spine.

In the early 1900's the Spaghetti Warehouse was built as a second branch of the popular Dallas chain Diesel-Boettcher warehouse. The highlight of the warehouse were several antique pieces that gave it a very classical look. For instance, a beautiful stairway from a European castle was placed in the restaurant.

Many people who believe in demons and spirits always

advise you against picking up antiques from abandoned castles and buildings. They believe that the spirits in these buildings usually latch on to the objects of the homes they live in. When you carry it into your space, it is almost like you are allowing these spirits in.

This makes them stay with you for longer and makes it harder for you to get rid of them. This is probably why the Spaghetti Warehouse soon turned into the most haunted place in Texas. The hauntings at the Spaghetti Warehouse became extremely popular and everyone was talking about it.

It was also in the news and people shared every bit of information that they had about the place. Manager, Sandra McMasters who worked for over a decade in this restaurant states that the building that the warehouse is now in used to be a pharmacy. The owner of this pharmacy died a very unnatural death. He fell down the elevator shaft and died. However, it is surprising that his spirit does not haunt the place.

Instead, his heart broken wife is the one who lurks around in the corridors. She died exactly a year after the pharmacist after she was unable to console her broken heart. Many visitors claim to have had paranormal experiences at the Spaghetti Kitchen. There are many people who actually visit the space just to experience the hauntings.

The second floor appears to be the area with the greatest ghostly activity. There is an antique trolley car which is located here. In addition to that, an urn cabinet has been kept here for several years. The incidents have been so bizarre and scary that the second floor remains closed for most of the year.

The lights are kept off and occasionally, visitors are allowed to make their way onto this scary floor. The second floor is also opened on some special occasions. It is known to be extremely eerie as you have the sensation of an additional presence while you walk down the corridors.

People who have worked in the Spaghetti Warehouse on a long term basis refuse to talk about it. They have had encounters with the spirits that they find too scary to even talk about. There is one waitress who is brave enough to talk about one of her scary experiences. The waitress, named Patti always used to find it hard to manage her shoe laces. They always seemed to come undone.

One day, one of her co workers brought it to Patti's

attention that her shoelaces were stretched out and were floating in thin air, as if someone was holding them at the ends. Patti simply said, " I hope I do not step on anyone." The shoe laces dropped immediately and Patti never had any trouble with her shoe laces again.

The upper floors are supposed to be so haunted that the staff refuse to venture into them. Like I mentioned before, spirits associate them with objects and stay with them. The urn cabinet that is placed on the second floor was previously used in orphanages. Now, the remains of these children are stored in the cabinet as there was no space to bury them.

While the urns are no longer in the cabinet, the spirits of these children still hold on. That is why you can distinctly hear the sounds of children crying and talking in the upper floors of the warehouse. It seems like there are several children out there who are just being children, playing and talking.

However, the staff and the visitors do not want anything to do with the haunting voices of these children that almost seem to beg for some attention. Manager McMasters, too, believes that the antiques in the warehouse are responsible for the paranormal activities in the space.

It appears to her that these spirits have been unwillingly brought to the warehouse. They are stranded and trapped here and as they look for a way to escape, they have encounters with the people at the restaurant. The spirits in the warehouse may have spooked several visitors but the staff say that they have never caused any harm.

It is just the regular poltergeist activity that the people in the warehouse have experienced. However, most members of the staff find something very amiss about the whole building. They are always on their guard and make it a point to enter the space after the sun is up and bright and never stay back too late into the night.

They do not even enter the building alone and wait for other staff members to be present. The idea that something is definitely around is spooky enough to make them all feel this way. Not one person has been harmed to date by any of the spirits. But they have all had their share of sightings and experiences that have made them weary of the building.

One waitress claims that she saw an antique wicker basket float around in the corridor and then just settle gently back on the floor. Another one claims that a wine bottle floated

50

mid air on to another table. It seemed like someone just carried it across to the other table. Most of them have heard their names being called out from rooms that are empty.

The ghost of the pharmacist's wife seems to be the one that causes the most trouble around the warehouse. She actually walks around the corridors sobbing and crying out loud at times. Several waiters say that they are unable to leave silverware neatly arranged. The minute they take their eyes off it, it is a mess.

Some guests have been tapped on their shoulder with no one standing behind them. Others have had their hair pulled really hard. These guests never returned. Would you if your hair was pulled as you enjoyed a pleasant Italian meal and you couldn't see the person who did it?

There have also been several unlucky (or lucky) guests who have had no such experiences at all. But the tales that the staff have to tell are so compelling that you are forced to believe in the legend of the Spaghetti Warehouse.

Manager McMasters recalls one such incident after which she never dared to work in the warehouse alone. She came in early one Saturday morning to get business rolling. She was welcomed by a gentleman who was pacing around the men's room.

Then, she heard loud voices coming out of the kitchen. These voices grew louder and she was able to hear the cooler doors opening and slamming shut. A freaked out McMasters ran out immediately and informed a policeman about what she had just experienced. He came in with a German Shepherd.

But neither the dog nor the police officer were able to detect anything. Everything in the warehouse was left where it was and it looked like no one had even been in the place until then. So, who was that gentleman. McMasters never saw him again and she never wishes to experience what she did that night.

Many testimonies shared by the staff on different occasions have been eerily similar. There have been several press releases that support the stories of these encounters. No one knows why this building is so haunted. But, many have attributed it to the fact that there are so many antique pieces in the building.

So, the next time you go out into a second hand store or decide to pick up a secondhand car, make sure you learn everything about whatever you bring back. You never know if you are bringing home more than just a snazzy car.

Chapter 7:

The Tillmore House

Popularized as the Tillmore house but originally known as the Summerwind house, this mansion is considered one of the most haunted houses in Wisconsin. What used to be a grand mansion is now demolished due to the horrifying tales that surrounded the house.

It is just a memory today, but a memory that haunts many and reminds them of the fearsome history of the mansion. The legend of Summerwind in Wisconsin has been told by many and each tale is stranger than the other, earning this house the title of the most haunted house in Wisconsin.

This huge mansion was built in the year 1916 by a man named Robert P Lamont. The house was built to serve as a summer home for him and his family. This house was skilfully placed on the shores of a lake so it could catch the cool breeze that blew across the lake providing the residents some relief from the scorching sun.

It was a very beautiful estate that was extremely relaxing.

Many people even believe that Mr. Lamont lived a very comfortable life in this mansion, so the stories about it being haunted could be mostly false. However, there is a story about Mr. Lamont that will make all the doubts disappear.

Mr. Lamont once had a very close encounter with a spirit who lived in the house. The apparition seemed so real to him that he actually fired bullets at it assuming that it was an intruder. The holes from the bullets could still be seen in the basement door right up until the time the house was demolished.

There is photographic evidence to suggest that this encounter was, in fact true. The family continued to live there until the death of Robert Lamont, however. But, there were no significant encounters with the dead besides this one. When Robert Lamont died, the house was sold several times. During the period that the house was vacant, people say that it was heavily damaged by the ghosts.

During the 1970's Arnold Hinshaw, his wife and six children moved into the house. They did not live in the house for too long, just six months. But, these six months would be the most dreadful ones that they would ever experience. Before the house was bought by this family, it was vacant for a long time.

This is when they had several intruders from the other world who had made it their home. The family often reported sightings of strange apparitions and shadows. The voices that they heard in the house seemed to be muffled and would stop immediately when someone entered the room.

One of the scariest apparitions that they spoke about was that of a woman who just hovered back and forth near the large French doors by the dining room. Sometimes they tried to convince themselves that these were just figments of their imagination.

However, when the visions became recurrent, they realized that they were not alone in that house. Several appliances broke down and just repaired themselves when they called upon a serviceman.

Windows and doors that had been latched shut would suddenly open and swing around violently. It was so bad that Arnold had to drive heavy nails through all the windows to keep them shut. In another instance, when Arnold headed out to the garage to take the car out and drive to work, it just burst into flames before him.

The source of the fire was never found and it was likely that nothing around the car or in it was the reason for this sudden explosion. Despite these eerie events, the family continued to stay there. They even decided to get the house renovated.

However, most of these workers would never turn up for work and would have the strangest excuses for it. It was the haunted reputation of the house that scared most of these workers away. Ultimately, the Hinshaws decided that it was up to them to have the house renovated. They started doing all the work themselves and would soon be part of many experiences that would change their perception of the house forever.

While painting the closet in one of the bedrooms, Arnold discovered that there was a large shoe drawer on the back wall of the closet. When he took the drawer off, he saw that it camouflaged a very large space that was dark and narrow. He wanted to check what this passage led to.

When he squeezed in with a torch he found a corpse jammed into the narrow space. They tried to convince themselves that this was the corpse of an animal that had crawled in. Then, they had their little child investigate. She crawled in and began to scream in horror.

It was a human corpse and she brought out a skull that still had portions of dark hair stuck to it. They also uncovered a rotting arm and a portion of a human leg. The Hinshaws were too frightened to even call the authorities about this body. So, it is unknown if the story was concocted to make the house seem haunted or whether the body had actually been uncovered by the child.

In any case, it is too long ago for anyone to investigate. So, people believe whatever they choose to believe. What is true are the rest of the incidents that the family encountered in the house. Arnold used to regularly play the Hammond organ in the house as he was fond of it.

But, after the body had been uncovered, the stuff he played seemed to be way out of tune and just a random mixture of notes and sounds. It was so eerie that the family begged him to stop. He just said that the demons in his head wouldn't let him.

Arnold's organ playing became more frenzied each day, forcing the whole family to huddle up in the bedroom, cowering in fear. Arnold had a mental breakdown then and his wife even tried to kill herself.

Arnold's health deteriorated day after day and there were no hope of his recovery. Eventually, his wife remarried and moved out of the house only to discover that her father would soon buy the mansion. She was horrified as they did not know about the events that had transpired in the house. Her parents wanted to convert this space into a restaurant and inn.

Despite their daughter begging and pleading, the Bobers decided to buy the place. Mr. Bober eventually discovered that the house was haunted but this wasn't enough to scare him away. He spent several days in the house trying to identify the spirit. Ultimately, he discovered that the place was haunted by a man named Jonathan Carver.

Carver was a British explorer who was on the lookout for a deed given to him by Sioux Indians. Through dreams and through the Ouija board, Carver communicated with Bober and asked for his help to find the deed. Bober even wrote a book called the CARVER EFFECT to narrate his communication with the dead explorer.

Bober was told that the deed was sealed into the foundation of the house. He began to look for it with his son and son in law. They pulled the closets apart to look for this deed. That is when Ginger mentioned the dark passage they had uncovered behind the closet.

The men climbed into the passage and looked around. To their surprise, the corpse was gone. No one knows if this body was removed by someone else or a supernatural force. Or were all the things that Arnold and his family witnessed imaginary?

Bober's son went back into the house towards the end of that season. He wanted to get some repair work done and also get rid of the bats and pests that had invaded the space while it was vacant. He had to close the windows as it began to pour that night.

When he walked upstairs, he heard some sounds from the hallway. These voices called his name out and he heard two loud gun shots. It seemed like someone had just fired a gunshot inside the house as it reeked of gunpowder. The kitchen was also filled with smoke as if the incident had just occurred.

He examined the entire place but found no one there. That is when he saw the bullet holes in the basement door. These bullet holes were old worn out ones and not fresh. How could it be that someone just fired a bullet but there were no traces of the bullet itself?

And, there were two shots that he heard. Just as many as the first owner of the house had fired at the apparition. Could there be a connection? Bobers son left the house in the afternoon and decided to continue with the construction work the following day.

The Bobers realized that turning this house into a restaurant would not be the easiest task. The workmen simply refused to stay in the building and felt like they were always being watched by someone. They felt uneasy in the house and felt like the presence followed them from one room to the other.

Another thing they discovered was that the house actually expanded and shrunk overnight. The Bobers would measure the house and the size would be entirely different the next day. Once, Mr. Bober measured the seating area and figured that at least 150 people could be seated there. However, the very next day, he found that they could seat less than half that number.

Several pictures were taken during this renovation period. The space looked entirely different in each of the images. Once, Mr. Bober saw curtains in the pictures; Curtains that he himself had removed before taking those pictures.

These incidents made everyone believe that the house perhaps had some distorted element of time within itself.

Now, could the two gun shots heard by Mr. Bober's son be an instance of events repeating themselves? How could the pictures and the actual space look so different from one another? Or did the things like the voices signify something that would happen in the future?

The project of building a restaurant was abandoned by the Bobers eventually. Although Mr. Bober did communicate with the spirit of Carver, he never even spent a night alone in the house. He would rather sleep in the RV that was parked outside.

He explained that Carver did not want anyone to live in the house or renovate it until the deed was found. This deed which prevented Jonathan Carver from resting even after his death was never to be found. What it contained and why it meant so much to him will never be known.

The claims made by the Bobers have often been questioned due to their bizarre nature. People never really knew if he even owned the house. Irrespective of what the truth behind the Summerwind Mansion is, most people have been too terrified to talk about it. What the Hinshaws saw was not of this world.

How could someone be driven to the point of insanity so suddenly? It seemed like there was someone or something that was trying to communicate with the residents of this house. As Mr. Bober claimed, why was the deed so important to someone that he would seek assistance from the other world just to find it?

What is even scarier is the fact that people who lived in this house were actually able to experience the shift between the dimensions of time. One house did make people go into the future in one instant and then send them rushing back to the past the next second. What could the mystery behind these strange occurrences be?

Only the people who moved into the house could tell. One thing was sure, everyone who lived there knew from the first day that they were not alone. How about you? Is someone watching you right now?

Chapter 8:

The Ancient Ram Inn, Gloucestershire, England

The aura around the ancient Ram Inn is very chilling. The presence of the Inn itself is so eerie that people will not even walk past it after the sun has set . The building was constructed in the year 1145 and it was used as housing for the laborers who were involved in building the Parish church, St Mary's right outside the Inn.

The priest lived in this building for many years before it was converted into an inn and restaurant. It was in business as an inn until 1968. This building was then purchased by a man named John Humphries. There have been no occupants of the house ever since and Humphries is still trying to keep the structure intact.

He has had several instances of former residents interfering in issues related to the house. In addition to that, the inn gained the reputation of being extremely haunted.

Those who enter the inn for the first time feel a very foreboding aura. The walls are bare and the floorboards creak with every step that you take.

The staircases are very steep and you will see some strange shadows on the wall. Whether this can be attributed to the construction of the building or whether these shadows are a reflection of the building's past is still something that people debate. There are several stories about the haunted past of this building that can send shivers down the spine of even the most ardent cynic of ghost stories.

One visitor describes the inside of the Ram Inn as dark and heavy. When you enter, the first room that you will see is the Men's Kitchen. It is believed that this kitchen has been constructed on the burial ground of pagan worshipers. You can often hear the sound of a baby crying in this room.

The next spot in the house that most visitors find particularly disturbing is the stairway. It is dark and steep to begin with and many visitors claim that they have been pushed off the stairs by invisible forces.

In June 1999, a picture of the stairway was taken. This picture showed a strange white mist that looked about the height of an adult human climbing up the stairs. This is the image that attracted people to the inn from far and wide. The first floor houses the Bishop's room which is considered to be the most haunted room.

A medium was once called to explore the room and learn why it was so terrifying. Just as the medium opened the door he was flung across the corridor. People say that the atmosphere in this room is nothing short of oppressive.

There is a dressing table in this room where a cavalier often appears. This apparition strides across the corridors when there is an onlooker. Many have seen the apparition of two monks in a certain corner of the house as well. One of the most terrifying encounters is with a man who appears screaming loudly.

He was murdered in the room apparently in a very cruel manner. His head was thrust into the fire and he still screams in pain to this day. When you get into the attic the oppressive aura turns melancholic. This is where one of the inn keeper's daughter was murdered in the 16th century.

People who have tried to sleep in the Bishop's room claim that they heard something very heavy being dragged across the floor. This is one haunted space that people do not doubt the authenticity of. It is easy to believe that the Inn is still haunted. The demons that exist in this inn are still very active and some are even malicious.

If you are fainthearted, this is one place that you certainly want to avoid. But if you want to experience the presence of the unknown world, this is the place to go to. There is always a chance that you will hear a sound or even see an image that you will never be able to get out of your head. This is where the dead have been walking amongst they living through night and day, for several centuries.

Chapter 9:

Chateau de Brissac, Maine-et-Loire, France

(https://www.flickr.com/photos/sybarite48/10672714816
/)

The Chateau de Brissac in Maine-et-Loire, France looks like a castle straight out of a fairy tale. It is a beautiful monument that is surrounded by sprawling gardens. In addition to that, the clear blue skies make this chateau look like something you would imagine princes and princesses live in.

Until the 15th century, this monument was a castle that was turned into a Chateau by King Rene. He had several castles altered to become chateaus. Of them all, the Brissac is considered to be the most beautiful. This is also one of the tallest structures in all of France.

But, to those who enter the walls of this castle, the world that they witness is right out of their worst nightmares. The chateau was destroyed during the 1790s after which it was rebuilt. The monument was subjected to several attacks, including the Huguenots, the Nordics, the English and even the Jacobin's.

It survived through all of that and has seen various generations come and go. All the residents were haunted by one particular entity. A tragic double murder took place in the 15th century, which left the chateau haunted. The residents named this entity *La Dame Verte* Or the 'Green Lady'.

This castle was constructed by King Philip II of France. When the English were defeated by the French, the property was given away to Guillaume des Roches. After this the Castle was rebuilt in the 15th century by Pierre de Breze who was King Charles II's chief minister.

His son, Jacques inherited the property and then married Charlotte of France. Their marriage was not a happy one. Charlotte was born to Agnes Sol and Charles VII illegitimately. Agnes Sol was an employee of King Rene. Despite the situation in which she was born, King Louis XI, the son of Charles VII loved his half sister dearly.

It is believed that Charlotte's adultery was the cause of a rift between her and her husband. One night when Jacques walked into the bedroom, he saw Charlotte in the arms of her own huntsmen. This enraged Jacques, so much that he slaughtered the couple there and then.

There is another story which states that he strangled his unfaithful wife in the Chapel Tower of the Chateau. There are several such stories, but no one knows what exactly happened that night. Lady Charlotte and her lover were never seen after that that though.

Her half brother, Louis XI vowed to avenge the strange disappearance of his beloved sister. He ensured that Jacques was arrested the very next day and thrown into prison for several years to come. He had even convinced the court to sentence him to death. Jacques pleaded for mercy.

He did live, but all his property was seized. It was transferred to Jacques' son Louis. Just three years later though, the property was restored to Jacques by the successor of Louis XI.

In the 15th Century, the Crosse family took over the chateau. They were given the title of Dukes of de Brissac. To this day, the dukes still inhabit the chateau. All the generations that have lived in this Chateau have had encounters with the apparition of the Green Lady.

She walks around near the tower room of the chapel. This ghost has startled the guests of the Chateau and has also kept the various residents in terror. The lady gets her name because of the green gown that she wears.

Her face is supposed to be terrifying as it looks like the face of a decaying corpse. Instead of eyes and a nose, there are just gaping holes in her skull. She continues to walk around the castle and mourns her own tragic death. People have heard the loud moans of this lady who met such a cruel end for being unfaithful.

Chapter 10:

Lorgnette (The Haunted Vicarage)

Since the 1920's a small village called Borgavattnet in Sweden has been the center of several hauntings. The old vicarage that was built here in 1876 is considered to be the most haunted building of them all. People who visited this vicarage were unable to spend even one night there. It is reported that they fled the place screaming, in the middle of the night.

The haunting of the vicarage was documented by chaplain Nils Hedlund in the form of letters. These letters date back to 1927, the time when he lived in the house. The successor of Hedlund, Rudolf Tangden claimed that he saw the ghost of a woman walking around the house in the year 1930.

The same apparition was seen by his successor 10 years later. He and his wife have witnessed several paranormal activities including scary voices, objects levitating and even shadows on the walls.

In the year 1941, the vicarage had a visitor. This lady was asleep in the guestroom and woke up in the middle of the night with the scary sensation of being watched. When she looked around she saw three women sitting on the sofa staring at her. Terrified, she turned the lights on only to find them still sitting there. Only this time, they looked a little more blurry.

After this incident, the vicarage did not have any residents or visitors for a long time. In the year 1945, chaplain Erik Lindgren took up residence. He, too, had several encounters with the paranormal beings in the house. He wanted to make lengthy documents of all his encounters.

To do this comfortably, he even bought himself a rocking chair. However, whenever he sat down to write down the details of his encounters, he was thrown out of the chair by a powerful, invisible force.

The vicarage was investigated by several paranormal experts. One such investigation was aired on the first episode of Ghost Hunters in January 2009. Attempts to relieve the village of these activities were first made in the year 1981 by a controversial priest named Tore Forslund.

He tried to work against the occult phenomenon in the village as well. However, when all his attempts failed, he decided to leave the Church of Sweden. The vicarage is considered to be the most publicized haunted building in Sweden. There were several eerie sounds like footsteps and taps that were heard in the hall way.

Doors squeaked and you could even hear the sound of someone taking off a coat. These visitors walked in and out from dusk until dawn. Sometimes they even got violent and pushed people out of chairs and beds. They even sat next to you staring with cold, dead eyes.

Hedlund wrote in his letters about one particular incident that made it clear that the house was haunted. One day, when he was helping his wife clean up, he felt a very strange presence in the house. He ignored it and went about his chores. After all his work was done, he decided to go and take his laundry down from the clothesline.

All the clothes had been torn to shreds. He looked around to confirm whether it was an animal or someone playing a trick on them. When he discovered that it was neither, it became certain that they were sharing their home with someone else.

Sometimes, we live among those whom we have never known. While they stay with us, quietly observing our each and every move we are oblivious to the fact that they are right there next to us. It takes a dramatic manifestation like this to make us aware of the beings that we share our world with.

Never take the space that you live in for granted. People who have encountered these paranormal activities will tell you how terrifying it can be when you suddenly experience it. Just stay still and feel the air. Can you hear the breathing of someone else besides your own?

Conclusion

Thank you again for purchasing this book!

I hope this book was able to help you to gain an insight into the minds and the lives of these people who have seen a lot more than we can imagine in their lifetime. Their interactions with the paranormal remind us constantly not to take the lives that we have for granted.

Sometimes, all it takes is a new object in your home to turn your life upside down. So, be careful about the choices you make. Ask yourself when you are alone in your room if you are really the only one there?

The stories in these books are more than urban legends. People who lived in these homes are still alive to tell your their stories of horror. Some of them have even written books to document their lives and experiences.

These books are all available for us to read and help us understand a world that we often prefer to hide under cynicism and mockery. Ask yourself now, after you have read these accounts. Do you believe in ghosts?

If you enjoyed this book, would you be kind enough to leave me a review on Amazon? Just search for this title and my name on Amazon to find it. Thank you so much, it is very much appreciated!

Other Books Written By Me

Below you'll find some of my other popular books that are popular on Amazon and Kindle as well. You can visit my author page on Amazon to see other work done by me. (Max Mason Hunter).

Unexplained Phenomena

Unexplained Phenomena – Book 2

Bizarre True Stories

True Paranormal

True Paranormal – Book 2

True Ghost Stories And Hauntings

True Ghost Stories And Hauntings – Book 2

True Ghost Stories And Hauntings – Book 3

True Paranormal Hauntings

True Paranormal Hauntings – Book 2

True Paranormal Hauntings – Book 3

True Paranormal Hauntings – Book 4

If the links do not work, for whatever reason, you can simply search for these titles on the Amazon website with my name to find them.

LIBRARY BUGS
BOOKS

Like FREE books?

Would you like them delivered to you every week?

Do you like non-fiction books on a huge range of different topics?

We send out FREE e-books every week so we can share our books with the world!

We have FREE books every week on AMAZON that we send to our email list. If you want in, then visit the link below to sign up and sit back and wait for new books to be sent straight to your inbox!

It couldn't be simpler!

www.LibraryBugs.com

If you want FREE books delivered straight to your inbox, then visit the link above and soon you'll be receiving a great list of FREE e-books every week!

Enjoy :)

9 781530 531516